Technical Services Manager; Project Manager; Line Practical Job Interview Questions & Answers for Technology Service Manager

A WORD FROM THE AUTHOR:

It has precisely articulated bottom line practical real interview questions with answers to be successful at any Technical Services Manager Job interview. It will help you to convey powerful and useful information to the employer successfully. It will provide Technical Services Manager professionals all the theoretical and practical aspects of Technical Services knowledge so that they can Architect, implement, operate, manage, and integrate enterprise IT systems and infrastructure.

Practicing with this interview questions and answers in the mirror will help with your replies to questions and pass with flying colors. It also covers non-technical, HR and Personnel questions in brief. Practicing with this interview questions and answers in the mirror will help with your replies to questions and pass with flying colors.

Good Luck,

Peter Alter

*****

It's for the following job interviews:
Technical Services Manager
Technical Services Mgr.
Technical Services Manager
ITIL/IT Service Management
IT Service Desk Manager
IT Service Delivery Consultant
Sr Account Manager

You will learn to practice mock interviews and answer Technical Services Mgr. Interview Questions you'll Most Likely Be Asked:

- Develop processes to comply with company policies
  - Establish best practices and standard procedures
  - Determines root cause of issues
  - Organize and ensure subject matter expertise and cross training
  - Build training material and organizes training discussions for staff
  - Create documented procedures for PC distribution
  - Provide input to company policies
  - Desktop rollout projects
  - Develop continuous process improvements
  - Research technologies to improve end user service
  - Work with other IT organizations to improve service processes
  - Manage SLA's and performance metrics
  - IT asset policies and data security
  - Proactive and Reactive Problem Management
  - Trend Analysis
- Conduct and facilitate RCA (Root Cause Analysis)
- Develop, operate and maintain the IT infrastructure
- Define and maintain technology and integration models
- Manage day-to-day IT operations.
- Maintain availability of computer systems
- Provision of IT infrastructure services
- Procure, develop and maintain a disaster recovery plan.
- Develop and control the IT security policy.
- Identify and recommend opportunities for improving technical infrastructure
- Business continuity planning for mission critical applications
- Ownership of all customer incidents, problems or service requests
- Management of all SLA's and quality standards.
- Customer Incident and Escalation Management
- Customer Relationship Management and Service Reviews.
- Manage Third Party Suppliers.
- Service Desk Knowledge Management.

Communication & Process Improvement.
Oversees requests, incidents and problems
Manage and coordinate urgent complicated support issues
Act as escalation point for all requests and incidents

Copy Right
BLGS LLC
Pennsylvania, USA

All rights reserved. No part of this may be used or reproduced in any form or by any means, or stored in a database or retrieval system, or transmitted or distributed in any form by any means, electronic, mechanical photocopying, recording or otherwise, without the prior written permission of author or publisher. The information provided is for only instructional value. This book is sold as is, without warranty of any kind, either expresses or implied. This e-book is provided "as is" without warranty of any kind, either express or implied, including, but not limited to, the implied warranties of merchantability, fitness for a particular purpose, or non-infringement. In no event shall the authors or copyright holders, publisher, distributor be liable for any claim, damages or other liability, whether in an action of contract, tort or otherwise, arising from, out of or in connection with the book or the use or other dealings in the book.

This publication could include technical inaccuracies or typographical errors. Changes are periodically added to the information herein; these changes will be incorporated in new editions of the publication. While every precaution has been taken in the preparation of this book, the publisher and the author assume no responsibility for errors or omissions. Neither is any liability assumed for damages resulting from the use of the information or instructions contained herein. It is further stated that the publisher and author are not responsible for any damage or loss to your data or your equipment that results directly or indirectly from your use of this book. All products mentioned in this book are trademarks, registered trademarks or service marks of the companies referenced in this book. This note is not sponsored, endorsed or affiliated by any associated vender. ITIL is a registered trademark of OGC. This note is not sponsored, endorsed or affiliated by any associated vender.

Information Technology Service Management/Technical Services Manager/ Service Delivery Manager/Project Manager Job Interview Questions?

Suggested Answers

What is ITIL?

The Information Technology Infrastructure Library (ITIL) is a framework of best practices.
The concepts within ITIL support information technology services delivery organizations with the planning of consistent, documented, and repeatable or customized processes that improve service delivery to the business.

ITIL framework consists of which processes?

1. Service Support (Service Desk, Incident Management, Problem Management, Change Management, Configuration Management, and Release Management)

2. Services Delivery (Service Level Management, Capacity Management, Availability Management, Financial Management and ITS Service Continuity Management).

Explain one benefit of ITIL?

The quality and the costs of the IT services can be controlled more efficiently.

What are the benefits of implementing a service desk?

1. Increased first call resolution
2. Improved tracking of service quality
3. Improved recognition of trends and incidents
4. Improved employee satisfaction
5. Skill based support

6. Rapidly restore service
7. Improved incident response time
8. Quick service restoration

What Processes are utilized by the Service Desk?

Workflow and procedures diagrams

What is the objective of Incident Management?

Minimize the disruption to the business by restoring service operations to agreed levels as quickly as possible.

What are the Benefits of an Incident Management Process?

1. Incident detection and recording
2. Classification and initial support
3. Investigation and diagnosis
4. Resolution and recovery

5. Incident closure
6. Incident ownership, monitoring, tracking and communication
7. Repeatable Process

What is the goal of Problem Management?

The object of problem management is to resolve the root cause of incidents, to minimize the adverse impact of incidents and problems on the business and secondly to prevent recurrence of incidents related to these errors.

What's the difference between problem and known error?

A `problem' is an unknown underlying cause of one or more incidents, and a `known error' is a problem that is successfully diagnosed and for which a work-around has been identified. The outcome of known error is a request for change (RFC).

When can the KE known error be closed?

When a review of the change has lead to a satisfactory result.

What is the purpose of Problem Management?

1. Identify potentially recurring incidents
2. Determine the root cause
3. Take steps to prevent the incidents from reoccurring.

What are the Phases in the overall Problem Management Process?

1. Detection and Logging
2. Prioritization and Planning
3. Investigation and Diagnosis
4. Resolution

Which ITIL process controls the flow of incident information?

Incident Management

When must a Post Implementation Review take place?

After every change.

What are IT Service Continuity Management responsibilities?

1. Analyzing risks.
2. Testing back-out arrangements.
3. Drawing up back-out scenarios.

Which ITIL process helps to monitor the IT services by maintaining a logical model of the IT infrastructure and IT services?

Configuration Management.

Explain Deming quality circle steps must to ensure good performance?

Plan-Do-Check-Act

Who is responsible for result of the process?

Process owner

Explain the difference between a process and a project?

A process is continuous and has no end date.
Project has a finite life span.

What is the basis of the ITIL approach to service management?

Interrelated Activities.

Explain Classification?

Its the process of formally grouping Configuration Items (CIs) by type, e.g. hardware, software, accommodation, people, documents, business processes, external services and it takes place immediately after recording and registering an incident.

What Information is regularly exchanged between Problem Management and Change Management?

RFCs resulting from known errors.

How Availability Management's manage the availability plan for current and future?

By using an emergency power provision

What's the importance of a service desk?

- The Service Desk is critically important as the very first contact the organization's users have with IT Services.
- This department also distributes information to users.

- It is responsible for tracking and monitoring an incident also.

What is incident management process? Examples?

Incident Management (IcM) is an IT service management (ITSM) process area
Its objective is to restore a normal service operation as quickly as possible
Incidents should be classified as they are recorded,

Examples:

    Application
        Service not available
        Application bug
        Disk-usage threshold exceeded
    Hardware
        System-down
        Automatic alert
        Printer not printing

What is Proactive problem management?

Finding potential problems and errors in an IT infrastructure before they cause incidents.

What's the difference between Incident, Problem and Known Error?

Incident => an incident is any event that is not part of the standard operation.
Example no frees space on user's hard disk.

Problem =>a problem is the unknown underlying cause of one or more incidents. Incident can never become a problem.

Known Error =>is an incident or problem for which the root cause is known and for which a temporary workaround or permanent alternative has been identified.
Request for Change (RFC) is needed in order to fix the known error.

What's the plan for Desktop rollout projects?

1. Evaluate
2. Plan
3. Build
4. Deploy
5. Operate

Which activity in the problem management process is responsible for generating Requests for Change (RFC)?

Error Control.

One of the tasks of Problem Management. Error Control encompasses identifying, recording, classifying and progressing Known Errors.

Which ITIL process is responsible to identify the cause?

Problem Management.

Which ITIL process provides change proposals in order to eliminate structural errors?

What's the goal of Problem Management?

As per ITIL the goal of Problem Management is to minimize the adverse impact of Incidents and Problems on the business that is caused by errors within the IT Infrastructure, and to prevent recurrence of Incidents related to these errors.

Problem Management tries to get to the root cause of Incidents and then initiate actions to improve or correct the situation.

When is a known error identified?

When the cause of the problem is known.

What is Problem Management?

ITIL process responsible for tracing the underlying cause of errors.

Give an example of proactive problem management?

Trend analysis, pain value analysis

How does problem management contribute?

By making a knowledge database available, it contributes

To a higher solution percentage of first-line support.

What is the primary task of error control?

Correcting known errors.

What is meant by urgency of an incident?

The degree to which the solution of an incident tolerates delay.

ITIL process Incident Management. Objective?

Restore normal state IT service operations as quickly as possible to minimize the adverse impact on business operations by correcting malfunctions in the services

While registering an incident what will be the first step?

Giving an incident number.

Which ITIL process has the task of classifying incoming interruption reports?

Incident Management

Who determines whether that an incident can be closed?

User

Technical expertise in the Incident Management process called?

Functional Escalation.

Reliability, Serviceability and Maintainability are components of which ITIL process?

Availability Management

What is serviceability?

The degree to which the provision of IT services can be supported by maintenance contracts.

What's "Mean Time To Repair" (MTTR)?

Average downtime of a service.

A report specifying the duration of an interruption of a configuration item is part of Which ITIL process manager?

Availability Manager

What is application sizing?

Determining the hardware capacity required to support new or adapted applications.

What part of the capacity management process verify CPU load for scheduling activity?

Demand Management

Capacity management responsible for what?

Resource management.

Capacity Management is responsible for determining the hardware necessary in order to support an application.

When the urgency of the change is determined?

After acceptance of a request for change

What is CMDB?

The database where are the statuses of changes recorded. The configuration management database. (CMDB)

Which ITIL process is responsible for replacing a defective PC?

Change Management

Who decides the category of a change?

The change manager.

Who is change manager?

CHANGE MANAGER controls the lifecycle of all Changes and takes a leadership in organizing a meeting where implementation plan is discussed.

Which change must be made quickly called?

An urgent change.

What defines a category for a change?

The consequences of the change e.g.: limited, substantial, significant, etc.

When Change management plays a coordinating role?

When implementing a new version of an application

What's RFC?

A request to replace something within the IT infrastructure

What is FSC (Forward Schedule of Changes)?

Forward Schedule of Change (FSC) is used to inform the recipients of the upcoming changes and the planning of changes are kept up to date in FSC.

What's Standard Change?

Fully described and approved change that does not have to be evaluated by change management each time.

How to prevent incidents resulting from changes to the IT infrastructure?

By Change Management

Which subject should be one of the standard items on the agenda of a meeting of the Change Advisory Board (CAB)?

Ongoing or concluded changes.

Which ITIL process is responsible for analyzing risks and counter measures?

IT service continuity management

Which ITIL process aims to trace business-critical services for which supplementary emergency measures must be taken?

IT Service Continuity Management

Which ITIL process carries out a risk analysis on the possible threats to and vulnerabilities of the IT infrastructure?

IT Service Continuity Management

Which aspects are described in a Service Level Agreement (SLA)

The quality expressed in quantity and costs of the services offered.

What aspects would you not expect to see in a Service level report designed for the customer?

The average utilization Level of the service desk

How can an organization determine the effectiveness of the Service Level Management process?

By measuring customer satisfaction.

Which ITIL process is responsible for creating the cost agreements for extra support of the service desk?

Service Level Management

After the evaluation of a service which activity takes place?

Adjusting of the service.

With aim of improving an IT service where are activities documented?

Service Improvement Program (SIP)

How to check IT infrastructure have been properly documented?

In Configuration Management

What is the difference between the Asset Management and Configuration Management?

Asset Management monitors aspects such as depreciation and configuration management monitors aspects such as the relationships between the configuration items.

What does the term 'detail level' mean in CMDB?

The depth of the database structure.

Which ITIL process includes the activity of describing and registering all components in the IT infrastructure?

Configuration management

What is a baseline in the IT infrastructure?

A standard configuration (such as a standard workstation)

Audits are regularly implemented for?

Verification

Which data, for a new configuration item (CI), is recorded in the configuration management database (cmdb)?

The relationship to other configuration items.

What is the criterion used by change management in determining the category for a request for change?

Impact

When is a back-out plan invoked?

When it is found that something went wrong when implementing a change.

What is the first activity when implementing a release?

Compiling the release schedule

Which process is responsible for ensuring this updated version is tested?

Release Management

What is Definitive Software Library?

Authorized versions of all software used on the infrastructure.

Software is checked for viruses before it goes into the Definitive Software Library (DSL).

What ITL process is responsible for ensuring that only virus-free software is put into the DSL?

Release Management

Which ITIL process is responsible for annually allocating the costs of underpinning contracts?

Financial Management for IT Services.

Which ITIL process is responsible for setting up the cost allocation system?

Financial Management for IT services.

Which activity in the ITIL process "Financial Management for IT Services" is responsible for billing the services that were provided to the customer?

Charging

Which ITIL process provides an insight, through the modelling activity, into trends that could cause performance problems in the future?

Capacity Management.

Which ITIL process has responsibility in preventing unauthorized access to data?

Security Management.

Where are agreements regarding security management recorded?

In a Service Level Agreement. (SLA)

Which ITIL process handles the implementation of the policy for access management and access to information systems and ensures specified information security requirements?

Security management

The correctness of data best describes the basic concept of integrity in which process?

Security management

When must a Post Implementation Review take place?

After every Change

Which activity is not the responsibility of IT service continuity management?

Executing impact analyses of incidents related to the back-out facilities

Which ITIL process has responsibility in preventing unauthorized access to data?

Security management

Which ITIL department has responsibilities that include distributing information to users?

Service desk

Where are activities documented with the aim of improving an IT service?

Service improvement program (SIP)

In the change management process, which role is ultimately responsible for the entire process?

Change Manager

What is an example of proactive problem management?

A trend analysis

Which data, for a new configuration item (CI), is recorded in the configuration management database (CMDB)?

The relationship to other configuration items

Which activity is not the responsibility of IT service continuity management?

Executing impact analyses of incidents related to the back-out facilities

Which ITIL process provides change proposals in order to eliminate structural errors?

Problem Management

Which activity is not a Service Desk activity?

Solving a Problem

What describes the basic concept of integrity in the Security Management process?

The correctness of the data

Which ITIL process responsible for annually allocating the costs of underpinning contracts?

Financial Management for IT services

How does Problem Management contribute to a higher solution percentage of first-line support?

By making a knowledge database available

Which activity is not a service Desk activity?

Solving a problem

Which statement best describes the role of the service Desk?

The service Desk functions as the first contact for the customer
Agreed IT service is available

When an organization decides to control the flow of incidents information within the IT organization, which ITIL process would it be putting in place?

Incident Management

How a change that must be made quickly is called?

An urgent change

To support an application Which ITIL process is responsible for determining the hardware necessary in order?

Capacity Management

Which subject should be one of the standard items on the agenda of a meeting of the Change Advisor Board (CAB)?

Ongoing or concluded changes

What is a benefit of using ITIL?

That the quality and the costs of the IT services can be controlled more efficiently

What is the basis of the ITIL approach to Service Management?

Interrelated activities

Who decides the category of a change?

The change manager

What criterion defines a category for a change?

The consequences of the change such as limited, substantial, significant etc

Which activity is responsible for generating requests for change (RFCs)?

Error Control

Which status is a problem assigned once its cause has been identified?

Known Error

Who is responsible for tracking and monitoring an incident?

Service Desk

What happens during monitoring?

Guarding agreements with the customer

Where are the statuses of changes recorded?

In the configuration management database (CMDB)

Which ITIL process is responsible for setting up the cost allocation system?

Financial Management for IT Services

What is a benefit of using ITIL?

Efficiently

What is the difference between a process and a project?

A process is continuous and has no end date, whereas a project has a finite lifespan

Software is checked for viruses before it goes into the Definite Software Library (DSL).

What ITIL process ensures virus-free software?

Release Management

Audits are regularly implemented in?

Verification

When must a Post Implementation Review take place?

After every Change

What does Mean Time to Repair (MTTR) mean?

Average downtime of a service

For what is capacity Management responsible?

Resource Management

When is a known error identified?

When the cause of the problem is known

What is the term used for a situation derived from a series of incidents with the same characteristics?

A problem

When the cause of one or more incidents is not known, additional resources are assigned to identify the cause. Which ITIL process is responsible for this?

Problem Management

Which ITIL process provides an insight, through the modelling activity, into trends that could cause performance problems in the future?

Capacity Management

Which ITIL process is responsible for analyzing risks and counter measures?

IT Service Continuity Management

What parties involved in an incident determines whether that incident can be closed?

User

What activity takes place immediately after recording and registering an incident?

Classification

What is the use of additional technical expertise in the incident management process called?

Functional escalation

Change that does not have to be evaluated by Change Management each time?

Standard Change

Of which ITIL process are reliability, serviceability and maintainability components?

Availability Management

Which ITIL process aims to prevent incidents resulting from changes to the IT infrastructure?

Change Management

Where the planning of changes is kept up to date?

The FSC (Forward Schedule of Changes)

What is a baseline in the IT infrastructure?

A standard configuration (such as a standard workstation)

A process is a logically coherent series of activities for a pre-defined goal. What is the process owner responsible for?

The result of the process

How can an organization determine the effectiveness of the Server Level Management Process?

By measuring customer satisfaction

What is the best description of the contents of the Definitive Software Library?

Authorized versions of all software used on the infrastructure

How can an organization determine the effectiveness of the Service Level Management process?

By measuring customer satisfaction

Which ITIL process ensures that the information that has been made available satisfies the specified information security requirements?

Security Management

What is the first step when registering an incident?

Assign an incident number

Where are agreements regarding Security Management recorded?

In a service Level Agreement (SLA)

What is the primary task of Error Control?

Correcting known errors

Where are activities documented with the aim of improving an IT service?

Service Improvement Program (SIP)

Security Management includes a number of sub-processes. Which activity of security management leads to a security sub-clause in the Service Level Agreement (SLA)?

Plan

What is the first activity when implementing a release?

Compiling the release schedule

What is a request to replace something within the IT infrastructure called?

Request for change

Which ITIL process is responsible for tracing the underlying cause of errors?

Problem Management

What does Mean Time to Repair (MTTR) mean?

Average downtime of a service

Which ITIL process carries out a risk analysis threats and vulnerabilities of the IT infrastructure?

IT service continuity management

Capacity Management processes?

1. Performance monitoring
2. Workload monitoring
3. Application Sizing ITIL
4. Resource forecasting
5. Demand forecasting
6. Modeling

What is the first activity when implementing a release?

Compiling the release schedule

What ITIL process is responsible for ensuring that only virus-free software is in DSL?

Release Management

Only authorized software should be accepted into the DSL, strictly
Controlled by Change and Release Management.

Which ITIL process is responsible for annually allocating the costs of Underpinning Contracts?

Financial Management for IT Services, IT Financial Management is the discipline of ensuring IT infrastructure is obtained at the most effective price (which does not necessarily mean cheapest), and calculating the cost of providing IT services so that an organization can understand the costs of its IT services.

Which ITIL process provides an insight, through the Modelling activity, into trends that could cause performance problems in the future?

Capacity Management

Which ITIL process has responsibility in preventing unauthorized access to data?

Security Management

Where are agreements regarding Security Management recorded?

In a Service Level Agreement (SLA)

What is Security Management?

It handles implementation of the policy for access management and access to information systems.

The goal of the Security Management

1. The realization of the security requirements defined in the Service Level Agreement (SLA) and other external requirements which are specified in underpinning contracts, legislation and possible internal or external imposed policies.

2. The realization of a basic level of security. This is necessary to guarantee the continuity of the management organization. This is also necessary in order to reach a simplified Service Level Management for the information security, as it happens to be easier to manage a limited number of SLAs as it is to manage a large number of SLAs.

Which ITIL process ensures that the information that has been made available satisfies the specified information security requirements?

Security Management

Explain Plan sub-process?

The Plan sub-process contains activities that in cooperation with the Service Level Management lead to the (information) Security section in the SLA.
Plan sub-process contains activities that are related to the underpinning contracts which are specific for (information) security.

Types of Release?

Delta
Only those CI's that have actually changed since last release are included.

Full
All components of the Release are built, tested, distributed and
Implemented together (whether they have changed or not).

Package
Individual Releases both Full and Delta are grouped together to
form a Package for release.

What's the Incident Management primary focus?

The primary focus of *INCIDENT MANAGEMENT,* a component in the *ITIL* Service Support area, is to restore services following an incident as quickly as possible

How will you prepare for IT Services Business Continuity Plan?

- Project Initiation and Control
- Risk Evaluation and Control
- Business Impact Analysis
- Developing Recovery Strategies
- Emergency Response and Operations
- Coordination with Public Authorities

What is Configuration Status Accounting?

It's a task of Configuration Management concerned with recording the state of a Configuration Item (CI) at any point in time, past, present or future

Explain Queuing theory?

The more work going through a system, the busier it gets linearly, but the response time gets worse non-linearly.

Explain Operational Level Agreements?

It's an agreement between an IT service provider and another part of the same Organization.

Problem Management Components?

1. Problem control
2. Error control
3. Management reporting

When a customer's enquiry is not clear what the Service Desk should do?

All incidents must be fully logged

Why SLA should contain definitions of terms?

To ensure that both the customer and IT can clearly understand the terms, SLA
Must be objectively and unambiguously defined.

If the correction of the root cause is not possible, what happens?

If the correction of the root cause is not possible, a Problem Record is created
and the error-correction transferred to Problem Management.

What is Hot Standby site?

A site that provides for fast recovery and restoration of services and is
Sometimes provided as an extension to the intermediate recovery provided by a
Third party recovery provider.

What are Business Impact and Risk Analysis?

The Business Impact Analysis (BIA) identifies Vital Business Functions (VBFs)
and their dependencies.

Explain Overheads?

The total of indirect materials, wages and expenses.

Service Capacity Management?

Should ensure that the type, pattern and typical Resource requirements of all services is understood.

How will an organization benefit from a business continuity plan?

It enables a speedy recovery of service after a disaster.

What is Change Management?

The Process responsible for controlling the Lifecycle of all Changes.

What is the Primary objective of Change Management?

The primary objective of Change Management is to enable beneficial Changes to be made, with minimum disruption to IT Services.

What is recorded as part of a Change Record?

Each change record documents the lifecycle of a single change.

Responsibility of the Release Management?

1. Define the release policies

2. Control of the Definitive Hardware Storage (DHS)
3. Distribute Software and Associated CIs
4. Carry out S/W audits (using CMDB)
5. Manage the software releases
6. Oversee build of the software releases
7. Control of the Definitive Software Library (DSL)

Explain Release Management Objectives?

Release Management is responsible for implementation and quality control of all
The hardware and software installed, it must work closely with Change
Management and Configuration Management to ensure CMDB is fully up-to-
Date that provides an accurate image of the configuration of the IT infrastructure.

Objectives:

1. Safeguard all software and related items
2. Ensure that only tested correct version of authorized software are in use
3. Ensure that only tested correct version of authorized hardware are in use
4. Right software, right time, right place
5. Right hardware, right time, right place

List the sequence of events for describing an incident lifecycle after the incident has occurred?

1. Detection
2. Diagnosis
3. Repair
4. Recovery
5. Restoration

What are the main components of Incident Life-Cycle?

1. Accept Service Event

2. Register and Consult the CMDB(Configuration Management Database)
3. Classification
4. Solve
5. Closure

Define Problem?

The undiagnosed root cause of one or more incidents.

Budgeting and accounting for IT services benefits?

Financial Management process introduces the concept of Budgeting,
Accounting and Charging for IT services delivered to the customers so it helps in improved financial forecasting.

What is the responsibility of Release Management?

Release Management is responsible for managing the

Organisation's rights and obligations regarding software

When is requesting an urgent change justified?

The change is needed to correct an error on a business critical system.

What is the prime responsibility of availability management?

To deliver a level of availability that enables customers to satisfy their business objectives.

ITIL Availability Management aims to define, analyze, plan, measure and improve all aspects of the availability of IT services.

Availability Management is responsible for ensuring that all IT infrastructure, processes, tools, roles etc are appropriate for the agreed availability targets.

What is CAB?

Change Advisory Board (CAB) is a group of people that advises the Change Manager in the Assessment, prioritization and scheduling of Changes.

Change Advisory Board consists of which members?

Problem Manager
Change Manager
Customer representatives

Explain the relation between call, problem and incident?

In ITIL, a call can have only one parent call.
An Incident can only have one parent Problem.
A parent can be linked to several children.
The parent Problem can be linked to several children Incidents.

Name products for Windows administration that incorporates many of the ITIL best practices?

Dell Remote Infrastructure Monitoring (RIM) platform

For systems management what you recommend for implementations of ITIL?

Dell KACE Family of Systems Management Appliances

What you suggest for optimal storage management?

Hitachi Storage Management Process Consulting Services (SMPC)

What you suggest for DB?

Oracle provides capabilities to support the ITIL Incident Management process.
Oracle Enterprise Manager provides several best approach capabilities to
Support the ITIL SLM process.

What do you suggest for Backup and Recovery?

Based on Information Technology Infrastructure Library (ITIL) processes, Symantec Managed Backup Services

Non-Technical/Personal/HR interview: Complimentary

Bottom Line Job interview?

Bottom-line: You will learn to answer any questions in such a way that you match your qualifications to the job requirements.

Interview Question?

Example response. Try to customize your answers to fit the requirements of the job you are interviewing for.

What are your greatest strengths?

    I. Articulate.
    II. Achiever.
    III. Organized.
    IV. Intelligence.
    V. Honesty.
    VI. Team Player.
    VII. Perfectionist.
    VIII. Willingness.
    IX. Enthusiasm.
    X. Motivation.
    XI. Confident.
    XII. Healthy.

XIII. Likeability.
XIV. Positive Attitude.
XV. Sense of Humor.
XVI. Good Communication Skills.
XVII. Dedication.
XVIII. Constructive Criticism.
XIX. Honesty.
XX. Very Consistent.
XXI. Determination.
XXII. Ability to Get Things Done.
XXIII. Analytical Abilities.
XXIV. Problem Solving Skills.
XXV. Flexibility.
XXVI. Active in the Professional Societies.
XXVII. Prioritize.
XXVIII. Gain Knowledge by Reading Journals.
XXIX. Attention to details.
XXX. Vendor management skills.
XXXI. Excellent Project Management skills.
XXXII. Self-disciplined.
XXXIII. Self-reliant.
XXXIV. Self-starter.
XXXV. Leadership.
XXXVI. Team-building.
XXXVII. Multitasking.
XXXVIII. Prioritization.
XXXIX. Time management.
XL. Can handle multiple projects and deadlines.
XLI. Thrives under pressure.

XLII. A great motivator.
XLIII. An amazing problem solver.
XLIV. Someone with extraordinary attention to detail.
XLV. Confident.
XLVI. Assertive.
XLVII. Persistent.
XLVIII. Reliable.
XLIX. Understand people.
L. Handle multiple priorities.
LI. Build rapport with strangers.

What are your greatest weaknesses?

I. I am working on My Management skills.
II. I feel I could do things on my own in a faster way without delegating it.
III. Currently I am learning to delegate work to staff members.
IV. I have a sense of urgency and I tend to push people to get work done.
V. I focus on details and think thru the process start to finish and sometimes miss out the overall picture, so I am improving my skills by laying a schedule to monitor overall progress.

Had you failed to do any work and regret?

I. I have No Regrets.

II. I am Moving on.

Where do you see yourself five years from now?

I. I am looking for a long-term commitment.
II. I see a great chance to perform and grow with the company.
III. I will continue to learn and take on additional responsibilities.
IV. If selected I will continue rise to any challenge, pursue all tasks to completion, and accomplish all goals in a timely manner.
V. I am sure if I will continue to do my work and achieve results more and more opportunities will open up for me.
VI. I will try to take the path of progression, and hope to progress upwards.
VII. In the long run I would like to move on from a technical position to a management position where I am able to smoothly manage, delegate and accomplish goals on time.
VIII. I want to Mentor and lead junior-to-mid level reporting analysts.
IX. I want to enhance my management experience in motivating and building strong teams.
X. I want to build and manage relationships at all levels in the organization.
XI. I want to get higher degree, new certification.

How Will You Achieve Your Goals?

Advancing skills by taking related classes, professional associations, participating in conferences, attending seminars, continuing my education.

Why are you leaving Your Current position?

I. More money
II. Opportunity
III. Responsibility
IV. Growth
V. Downsizing and upcoming merger, so I made a good, upward career move before my department came under the axe of the new owners.

Why are you looking for a new job?

I have been promoted as far as I can go with my current employer. I'm looking for a new challenge that will give me the opportunity to use my skills to help me grow with the company.

Why should I hire you?

I. I know this business from ground up.
II. I have Strong background in this Skill.
III. Proven, solid experience and track record.

IV. Highest level of commitment.
V. Continuous education on current technical issues.
VI. Direct experience in leading.
VII. Hands-on experience.
VIII. Excellent Project Management skills.
IX. Demonstrated achievements.
X. Knowledge base.
XI. Communications skills.
XII. Ability to analyze, diagnoses, suggests, and implements process changes.
XIII. Strong customer service orientation.
XIV. Detail oriented, strong analytical, organizational, and problem solving skill.
XV. Ability to interact with all levels.
XVI. Strong interpersonal, relationship management skills.
XVII. Ability to work effectively with all levels, cultures, functions.
XVIII. I am a good team player.
XIX. Extensive Technical experience.
XX. Understanding of Business.
XXI. Result and customer-oriented.
XXII. Strong communication skills.
XXIII. Good Project and Resource management skills.
XXIV. Exceptional interpersonal and customer service skills.
XXV. Strong analytical, evaluative, problem-solving abilities.
XXVI. Good management and planning skills.
XXVII. Good Time Management skills.
XXVIII. Ability to work independently.
XXIX. I've been very carefully looking for the jobs.
XXX. I can bring XX years of experience.

XXXI. That, along with my flexibility and organizational skills, makes me a perfect match for this position.
XXXII. I see some challenges ahead of me here, and that's what I thrive on.
XXXIII. I have all the qualifications that you need, and you have an opportunity that I want. It's a 100% Fit.

Aren't you overqualified for this position?

I. In My opinion in the current economy and the volatile job market overqualified is a relative term.
II. My experience and qualifications make me do the job right.
III. I am interested in a long term relationship with my employer.
IV. As you can see my skills match perfectly.
V. Please see my longevity with previous employers.
VI. I am the perfect candidate for the position.
VII. What else can I do to convince you that I am the best candidate? There will be positive benefits due to this. Since I have strong experience in this ABC skill I will start to contribute quickly. I have all the training and experience needed to do this job. There's just no substitute for hands on experience.

Describe a Typical Work Week?

I. Meeting every morning to evaluate current issues.
II. Check emails, voice messages.
III. Project team meeting.

IV. Prioritize issues.
V. Design, configure, implement, maintain, and support. Perform architectural design. Review and analysis of business reports.
VI. Conduct weekly staff meetings.
VII. Support of strategic business initiatives.
VIII. Any duties as assigned. Implementation.
IX. Monitor and analyze reports. Routine maintenance and upgrades.
X. Technical support.
XI. Deploy and maintain.
XII. Provide day-to-day support as required. Work with customers and clients.
XIII. Documentation.
XIV. Standard operating procedures.
XV. Tactical planning.
XVI. Determine and recommend.
XVII. Plan and coordinate the evaluation.
XVIII. Effective implementation of technology solutions.
XIX. To meet the business objectives.
XX. Participation in budget matters.
XXI. Readings to Keep Abreast Of Current Trends and Developments in the Field.

Are You Willing to Travel?

I. For the right opportunity I am open to travel.
II. I'm open to opportunities so if it involves relocation I would consider it.

Describe the pace at which you work?

  I. I work at a consistent and steady pace.
  II. I try to complete work in advance of the deadline.
  III. I am able to manage multiple projects simultaneously.
  IV. I am flexible with my work speed and try to conclude my projects on time.
  V. So far I have achieved all my targets
  VI. I meet or exceeded my goals.

How Did You Handle Challenges?

  I. Whenever the project got out of track I Managed to get the project schedules back on the track.
  II. Whenever there was an issue I had researched the issues and found the solutions.
  III. We were able to successfully troubleshoot the issues and solve the problems, within a very short period of time.

How do you handle pressure? Stressful situations?

  I. In personal life I manage stress by going to a health club.
  II. I remain calm in crisis.
  III. I can work calmly with many supervisors at the same time.
  IV. I use the work stress and pressure in a constructive manner.

V. I use pressure to stay focused, motivated and productive.
VI. I like working in a challenging environment.
VII. By Prioritizing.
VIII. Use time management
IX. Use problem-solving
X. Use decision-making skills to reduce stress.
XI. Making a "to-do" list.
XII. Site stress-reducing techniques such as stretching and taking a break.
XIII. Asked for assistance when overwhelmed.

How Many Hours Do You Work?

I enjoy solving problems and work as much as necessary to get the job done.
The Norm is 40 hour week.

Why are you the best person for the job?

I. It's a perfect fit as you need someone like me who can produce results that you need, and my background and experience are proof.
II. As you can see in My resume I've held a lot of similar positions like this one, and hence I am a perfect fit as all those experiences will help me here.
III. I believe this is a good place to work and it will help me excel.

What are you looking for in a position?

I. I'm looking for an opportunity where I may be able to apply my skills and significantly contribute to the growth of the company while helping create some advancement and more opportunities for myself.
II. It seems this organization will appreciate my contributions and reward my efforts appropriately to keep me motivated.
III. I am looking for job satisfaction and the total compensation package to meet My Worth that will allow me to make enough money to support my lifestyle.

What do you know about our organization?

I. This is an exciting place to work and it fits my career goals.
II. This company has an impressive growth.
III. I think it would be rewarding to be a part of such a company.

What are your short term goals?

I'd like to find a position that is a good fit and where I can contribute and satisfy my professional desires.

What Salary are you looking for?

  I. Please provide me the information about the job and the responsibilities involved before we can begin to discuss salary.
  II. Please give me an idea of the range you may have budgeted for this position.
  III. It seems my skills meet your highest standards so I would expect a salary at the highest end of your budget.
  IV. I believe someone with my experience should get between A and B.
  V. Currently I am interested in talking more about what the position can offer my career.
  VI. I am flexible but, I'd like to learn more about the position and your staffing needs.
  VII. I am very interested in finding the right opportunity and will be open to any fair offer you may have.

Tell me more about yourself.

  I. I'm an experienced professional with extensive knowledge.
  II. Information tools and techniques.
  III. My Education.
  IV. A prominent career change.
  V. Personal and professional values.
  VI. Personal data.
  VII. Hobbies.

VIII. Interests.
IX. Describe each position.
X. Overall growth.
XI. Career destination.

Why did you leave your previous job?

I. Relocation.
II. Ambition for growth.
III. This new opportunity is a better fit for my skills and/or career ambitions.
IV. To advance my career and get a position that allows me to grow.
V. I was in an unfortunate situation of having been downsized.
VI. I'm looking for a change of direction.
VII. I want to visit different part of the country I'm looking to relocate.
VIII. I am looking to move up the with more scope for progression.

What relevant experience do you have?

I have these XYZ related experience.
I have these skills that can apply to internal management positions et al.

If your previous co-workers were here, what would they say about you?

Hard worker, most reliable, creative problem-solver, Flexible, Helping

Where else have you applied?

I am seriously looking and keeping my options open.

What motivates you to do a good job?

Recognition for a job well done.

Are you good at working in a team?

Yes.

Has anything ever irritated you about people you've worked with?

I've always got on just fine with all my co-workers.

Is there anyone you just could not work with?

No.

Tell me about any issues you've had with a previous boss.

I never had any issues with my boss.

Any questions?

Please explain the benefits and bonus.
How soon could I start, if I were offered the job?

Why did you choose this career?

    I. Life style.
   II. Passion.
  III. Desire.
  IV. Interesting.
   V. Challenging.
  VI. Pays Well.
 VII. Demand.

What did you learn from your last job experience?

I gained experience that's directly related to this job.

Why is there a gap in your resume?

Because of Personal and family reasons I was unable to work for some time.
Unemployed.
Job hunt.
Layoffs.

How do you keep current and informed about your job and the industries that you have worked in?

    I. I pride myself on my ability to stay on top of what is happening in the industry.
    II. I do a lot of reading.
    III. I belong to a couple of professional organizations.
    IV. I have a strong network with colleagues.
    V. I take classes and seminars.
    VI. I have started and participated in many technical blogs.

Tell me about a time when you had to plan and coordinate a project from start to finish?

    I. I headed up a project which involved customer service personnel and technicians.
    II. I organized a meeting and got everyone together.

III. I drew up a plan, using all best of the ideas.
IV. I organized teams.
V. We had a deadline to meet, so I did periodic checks with various teams involved.
VI. After four weeks, we were exceeding expectations.
VII. We were able to begin implementation of the plan.
VIII. It was a great team effort, and a big success.
IX. I was commended by management for my managing capacity.

What kinds of people do you have difficulties working with?

I. I have worked in very diverse teams.
II. Diversity means differences and similarities with men and women from very diverse backgrounds and culture. It helps us grow as a human being.
III. The only difficulty was related to work related dishonesty by a person.
IV. He was taking credit for all the work our team accomplished.

What do you want to be in 5 years?

I hope to develop my management skills by managing a small staff.

Ideal career?

I. I would like to stay in a field of ABC.
   II. I have been good at ABC.
   III. I look forward to ABC.

Responsibilities?

I would expect expanded responsibilities that could make use of my other skills.

Dream job?

Includes all of the responsibilities and duties you are trying to fill. I also thrive in the fast changing environment where there is business growth.

Skills?

I was very pleased to develop the A, B, C skills that you are seeking

What sets you apart?

   I. Once I am committed to a job or project I take it with tremendous intensity.
   II. I want to learn everything I can.
   III. I am very competitive and like to excel at everything I do.

If the project not gone as planned?

Backup and identify precautions.

If unable to meet deadlines?

    I. Negotiate.
    II. Discussion.
    III. Restructure.
    IV. Redefine Optimum goal.
    V. Show a price structure.

Interpersonal skill?

    I. I had to learn to say no.
    II. Helpful to other staff.
    III. Help in return.

Improve?

In any job I hold I can usually find inefficiencies in a process, come up with a solution.

What do you feel has been your greatest work-related accomplishment?

   I. Implemented an idea to reduce expenses, raised revenues.
   II. Solved real problems.
   III. Enhanced department's reputation.

Have you ever had to discipline a problem employee? If so, how did you handle it?

Problem-solving skills, listening skills, and coaching skills.

Why do you want this position?

   I. I always wanted the opportunity to work with a company that leads the industry in innovative products.
   II. My qualifications and goals complement the company's mission, vision and values.
   III. I will be able to apply and expand on the knowledge and experience, and will be able to increase my contributions and value to the company through new responsibilities.

Why are you the best person for this job?

   I. I have extensive experience in XYZ (Skill they are looking for)
   II. I'm a fast learner.
   III. I adapt quickly to change.
   IV. I will hit the ground running.
   V. I'm dedicated and enthusiastic.
   VI. I'm an outstanding performer.
   VII. I may be lacking in this specific experience but I'm a fast learner and I'll work harder.

What about Technical writing?

   I. I can convert any complex technical information into simple, easy form.
   II. I can write reports to achieve maximum results.

How versatile you are? Can you do other works?

I am flexible and can adapt to any changing situations.

How do you manage time?

    I. I am very process oriented and I use a systematic approach to achieve more in very less time.
    II. I effectively eliminate much paperwork.

How do you handle Conflicts?

    I. I am very tactful;
    II. I avoid arguments and frictions and
    III. I establish trust and mutual understanding.

What kind of supervisory skills you have?

I. I make sure that everyone understands their responsibilities.
II. I try to be realistic in setting the expectations and try to balance the work among all.

Any Bad Situation you could not solve?

I've never yet come across any situation that couldn't be resolved by a determined, constructive effort.

Anything else?

　I. I am excited and enthusiastic about this opportunity
　II. I am looking forward to working with you.

End

INDEX

Information Technology Service Management/Technical Services Manager/ Service Delivery Manager/Project Manager: Last-Minute Bottom Line Practical Job Interview Preparation Questions & Answers

Information Technology Service Management/Technical Services Manager/ Service Delivery Manager/Project Manager Job Interview Questions?

What is ITIL?

ITIL framework consists of which processes?

Explain one benefit of ITIL?

What are the benefits of implementing a service desk?

What Processes are utilized by the Service Desk?

What is the objective of Incident Management?

What are the Benefits of an Incident Management Process?

What is the goal of Problem Management?

What's the difference between problem and known error?

When can the KE known error be closed?

What is the purpose of Problem Management?

What are the Phases in the overall Problem Management Process?

Which ITIL process controls the flow of incident information?

When must a Post Implementation Review take place?

What are IT Service Continuity Management responsibilities?

Which ITIL process helps to monitor the IT services by maintaining a logical model of the IT infrastructure and IT services?

Explain Deming quality circle steps must to ensure good performance?

Who is responsible for result of the process?

Explain the difference between a process and a project?

What is the basis of the ITIL approach to service management?

Explain Classification?

What Information is regularly exchanged between Problem Management and Change Management?

How Availability Management's manage the availability plan for current and future?

What's the importance of a service desk?

What is incident management process? Examples?

What is Proactive problem management?

What's the difference between Incident, Problem and Known Error?

What's the plan for Desktop rollout projects?

Which activity in the problem management process is responsible for generating Requests for Change (RFC)?

Which ITIL process is responsible to identify the cause?

Which ITIL process provides change proposals in order to eliminate structural errors?

What's the goal of Problem Management?

When is a known error identified?

What is Problem Management?

Give an example of proactive problem management?

How does problem management contribute?

To a higher solution percentage of first-line support.

What is the primary task of error control?

What is meant by urgency of an incident?

ITIL process Incident Management. Objective?

While registering an incident what will be the first step?

Which ITIL process has the task of classifying incoming interruption reports?

Who determines whether that an incident can be closed?

Technical expertise in the Incident Management process called?

Reliability, Serviceability and Maintainability are components of which ITIL process?

What is serviceability?

What's "Mean Time To Repair" (MTTR)?

A report specifying the duration of an interruption of a configuration item is part of Which ITIL process manager?

What is application sizing?

What part of the capacity management process verify CPU load for scheduling activity?

Capacity management responsible for what?

Capacity Management is responsible for determining the hardware necessary in order to support an application.

When the urgency of the change is determined?

What is CMDB?

Which ITIL process is responsible for replacing a defective PC?

Who decides the category of a change?

Who is change manager?

Which change must be made quickly called?

What defines a category for a change?

When Change management plays a coordinating role?

What's RFC?

What is FSC (Forward Schedule of Changes)?

What's Standard Change?

How to prevent incidents resulting from changes to the IT infrastructure?

Which subject should be one of the standard items on the agenda of a meeting of the Change Advisory Board (CAB)?

Which ITIL process is responsible for analyzing risks and counter measures?

Which ITIL process aims to trace business-critical services for which supplementary emergency measures must be taken?

Which ITIL process carries out a risk analysis on the possible threats to and vulnerabilities of the IT infrastructure?

Which aspects are described in a Service Level Agreement (SLA)

What aspects would you not expect to see in a Service level report designed for the customer?

How can an organization determine the effectiveness of the Service Level Management process?

Which ITIL process is responsible for creating the cost agreements for extra support of the service desk?

After the evaluation of a service which activity takes place?

With aim of improving an IT service where are activities documented?

How to check IT infrastructure have been properly documented?

What is the difference between the Asset Management and Configuration Management?

What does the term 'detail level' mean in CMDB?

Which ITIL process includes the activity of describing and registering all components in the IT infrastructure?

What is a baseline in the IT infrastructure?

Audits are regularly implemented for?

Which data, for a new configuration item (CI), is recorded in the configuration management database (cmdb)?

What is the criterion used by change management in determining the category for a request for change?

When is a back-out plan invoked?

What is the first activity when implementing a release?

Which process is responsible for ensuring this updated version is tested?

What is Definitive Software Library?

What ITL process is responsible for ensuring that only virus-free software is put into the DSL?

Which ITIL process is responsible for annually allocating the costs of underpinning contracts?

Which ITIL process is responsible for setting up the cost allocation system?

Which activity in the ITIL process "Financial Management for IT Services" is responsible for billing the services that were provided to the customer?

Which ITIL process provides an insight, through the modelling activity, into trends that could cause performance problems in the future?

Which ITIL process has responsibility in preventing unauthorized access to data?

Where are agreements regarding security management recorded?

Which ITIL process handles the implementation of the policy for access management and access to information systems and ensures specified information security requirements?

The correctness of data best describes the basic concept of integrity in which process?

When must a Post Implementation Review take place?

Which activity is not the responsibility of IT service continuity management?

Which ITIL process has responsibility in preventing unauthorized access to data?

Which ITIL department has responsibilities that include distributing information to users?

Where are activities documented with the aim of improving an IT service?

In the change management process, which role is ultimately responsible for the entire process?

What is an example of proactive problem management?

Which data, for a new configuration item (CI), is recorded in the configuration management database (CMDB)?

Which activity is not the responsibility of IT service continuity management?

Which ITIL process provides change proposals in order to eliminate structural errors?

Which activity is not a Service Desk activity?

What describes the basic concept of integrity in the Security Management process?

Which ITIL process responsible for annually allocating the costs of underpinning contracts?

How does Problem Management contribute to a higher solution percentage of first-line support?

Which activity is not a service Desk activity?

Which statement best describes the role of the service Desk?

When an organization decides to control the flow of incidents information within the IT organization, which ITIL process would it be putting in place?

How a change that must be made quickly is called?

To support an application Which ITIL process is responsible for determining the hardware necessary in order?

Which subject should be one of the standard items on the agenda of a meeting of the Change Advisor Board (CAB)?

What is a benefit of using ITIL?

What is the basis of the ITIL approach to Service Management?

Who decides the category of a change?

What criterion defines a category for a change?

Which activity is responsible for generating requests for change (RFCs)?

Which status is a problem assigned once its cause has been identified?

Who is responsible for tracking and monitoring an incident?

What happens during monitoring?

Where are the statuses of changes recorded?

Which ITIL process is responsible for setting up the cost allocation system?

What is a benefit of using ITIL?

What is the difference between a process and a project?

What ITIL process ensures virus-free software?

Audits are regularly implemented in?

When must a Post Implementation Review take place?

For what is capacity Management responsible?

When is a known error identified?

What is the term used for a situation derived from a series of incidents with the same characteristics?

When the cause of one or more incidents is not known, additional resources are assigned to identify the cause. Which ITIL process is responsible for this?

Which ITIL process provides an insight, through the modelling activity, into trends that could cause performance problems in the future?

Which ITIL process is responsible for analyzing risks and counter measures?

What parties involved in an incident determines whether that incident can be closed?

What activity takes place immediately after recording and registering an incident?

What is the use of additional technical expertise in the incident management process called?

Change that does not have to be evaluated by Change Management each time?

Of which ITIL process are reliability, serviceability and maintainability components?

Which ITIL process aims to prevent incidents resulting from changes to the IT infrastructure?

Where the planning of changes is kept up to date?

What is a baseline in the IT infrastructure?

A process is a logically coherent series of activities for a pre-defined goal. What is the process owner responsible for?

How can an organization determine the effectiveness of the Server Level Management Process?

What is the best description of the contents of the Definitive Software Library?

How can an organization determine the effectiveness of the Service Level Management process?

Which ITIL process ensures that the information that has been made available satisfies the specified information security requirements?

What is the first step when registering an incident?

Where are agreements regarding Security Management recorded?

What is the primary task of Error Control?

Where are activities documented with the aim of improving an IT service?

Security Management includes a number of sub-processes. Which activity of security management leads to a security sub-clause in the Service Level Agreement (SLA)?

What is the first activity when implementing a release?

What is a request to replace something within the IT infrastructure called?

Which ITIL process is responsible for tracing the underlying cause of errors?

What does Mean Time to Repair (MTTR) mean?

Which ITIL process carries out a risk analysis threats and vulnerabilities of the IT infrastructure?

Capacity Management processes?

What is the first activity when implementing a release?

What ITIL process is responsible for ensuring that only virus-free software is in DSL?

Which ITIL process is responsible for annually allocating the costs of Underpinning Contracts?

Which ITIL process provides an insight, through the Modelling activity, into trends that could cause performance problems in the future?

Which ITIL process has responsibility in preventing unauthorized access to data?

Where are agreements regarding Security Management recorded?

What is Security Management?

Which ITIL process ensures that the information that has been made available satisfies the specified information security requirements?

Explain Plan sub-process?

Types of Release?

What's the Incident Management primary focus?

How will you prepare for IT Services Business Continuity Plan?

What is Configuration Status Accounting?

Explain Queuing theory?

Explain Operational Level Agreements?

Problem Management Components?

When a customer's enquiry is not clear what the Service Desk should do?

Why SLA should contain definitions of terms?

If the correction of the root cause is not possible, what happens?

What is Hot Standby site?

What are Business Impact and Risk Analysis?

Explain Overheads?

Service Capacity Management?

How will an organization benefit from a business continuity plan?

What is Change Management?

What is the Primary objective of Change Management?

What is recorded as part of a Change Record?

Responsibility of the Release Management?

- Explain Release Management Objectives?
- List the sequence of events for describing an incident lifecycle
- after the incident has occurred?
- What are the main components of Incident Life-Cycle?
- Define Problem?
- Budgeting and accounting for IT services benefits?
- What is the responsibility of Release Management?
- When is requesting an urgent change justified?
- What is the prime responsibility of availability management?
- What is CAB?
- Change Advisory Board consists of which members?
- Explain the relation between call, problem and incident?
- Name products for Windows administration that incorporates many of the ITIL best practices?
- For systems management what you recommend for implementations of ITIL?

What you suggest for optimal storage management?

What you suggest for DB?

Non-Technical/Personal/HR interview: Complimentary

Bottom Line Job interview?

Interview Question?

What are your greatest strengths?

What are your greatest weaknesses?

Had you failed to do any work and regret?

Where do you see yourself five years from now?

How Will You Achieve Your Goals?

Why are you leaving Your Current position?

Why are you looking for a new job?

Why should I hire you?

Aren't you overqualified for this position?

Describe a Typical Work Week?

Are You Willing to Travel?

Describe the pace at which you work?

How Did You Handle Challenges?

How do you handle pressure? Stressful situations?

How Many Hours Do You Work?

Why are you the best person for the job?

What are you looking for in a position?

What do you know about our organization?

What are your short term goals?

What Salary are you looking for?

Tell me more about yourself.

Why did you leave your previous job?

What relevant experience do you have?

If your previous co-workers were here, what would they say about you?

Where else have you applied?

What motivates you to do a good job?

Are you good at working in a team?

Has anything ever irritated you about people you've worked with?

Is there anyone you just could not work with?

Tell me about any issues you've had with a previous boss.

Any questions?

Why did you choose this career?

What did you learn from your last job experience?

How do you keep current and informed about your job and the industries that you have worked in?

Tell me about a time when you had to plan and coordinate a project from start to finish?

What kinds of people do you have difficulties working with?

What do you want to be in 5 years?

Ideal career?

Responsibilities?

Dream job?

Skills?

What sets you apart?

If the project not gone as planned?

If unable to meet deadlines?

Interpersonal skill?

Improve?

What do you feel has been your greatest work-related accomplishment?

Have you ever had to discipline a problem employee? If so, how did you handle it?

Why do you want this position?

Why are you the best person for this job?

What about Technical writing?

How versatile you are? Can you do other works?

How do you manage time?

How do you handle Conflicts?

What kind of supervisory skills you have?

Any Bad Situation you could not solve?

Anything else?

End

About the authors/editor/compiler: Peter Alter is an author, educator, and an IT professional with over 18 years of experience in information technology.

The present edition of this book is a compilation of interview questions. It is hoped that it will be received well. Our efforts have been directed at making this note informative and useful for your interview, we will truly appreciate all forms of feedback. Please send your feedback to: bottomline@interview-guru.info
It is strongly recommended that you attend a
Formal and recognized training course and that you purchase and study the ITIL Service Delivery & Support texts. These materials are neither endorsed nor recognized by OGC. Our efforts have been directed at making this note informative and useful for your interview, we will truly appreciate all forms of feedback.
Disclaimer of Warranty, No Liability:
THE INFORMATION, CONTENTS, GRAPHICS, DOCUMENTS AND OTHER ELEMENTS INCLUDED HEREIN (COLLECTIVELY THE "CONTENTS") ARE PROVIDED ON AN "AS IS" BASIS WITH ALL FAULTS AND WITHOUT ANY WARRANTY OF ANY KIND.
Restrictions on use of content per Internet Privacy act.
The content is copyright © BLGS. BLGS is independent training provider. All rights reserved. You cannot reproduce by any methods such as linking, framing, loading positing to blogs et al, transfer, distribute, rent, share or storage of part or all of the content in any form without the prior written consent of BLGS .its solely for your own non-commercial use. You may not change or delete any proprietary notices from materials received. We assume no responsibility for the way you use the content provided. All these notes files on this site are here for backups for personal use only. If you are sharing any information from here with any third-party you are violating this agreement and Internet Privacy act. General Jurisdictional Issues: Terms of Use will be governed by the laws of the Bucks County in the state of Pennsylvania in USA without respect to its conflict of laws provision. You are responsible for compliance with applicable local laws.

Printed in Great
Britain
by Amazon